101 Ways

To Think Like a Business Person

Thinking with Purpose

Cindy Bahadur-Ramkumar

(B.A., Pg IIR, Lead Auditor HSEQ)

Copyright © 2015 by Cindy Bahadur-Ramkumar

All rights reserved. This book or any portion thereof may not be reproduced or used in any manner whatsoever without the express written permission of the author and publisher, except for the use of brief quotations in a book review or scholarly journal.

First Printing: 2015

ISBN-10: 1503263673
ISBN-13: 978-1503263673

DEDICATION

This book is dedicated to Entrepreneurs who:

Dare to DREAM BIG
Not afraid to FAIL
Determined without FEAR
and
CONQUER the world one step at a TIME.

To my family, my husband Neal and my three (3) kids Onalin, Milano and Alezandro, who dared to believe with me and supported me in this endeavour. Thank You.
Without your support and patience, I would never have been able to achieve all of my dreams.

Let this book be an inspiration to those who have ideas imprinted in their brain, but FEARFUL to action it, and afraid of its outcome.

THINK LIKE A BUSINESS PERSON. BE A BUSINESS PERSON.

ACKNOWLEDGMENTS

I am always grateful and always blessed to have the support of my family and friends.
My mom **Angela Bahadur** is my inspiration for this book, she was always proud of me. She spoke eloquently about me to everyone she met. Only as a mother myself, I now fully understand her meaning of a mom's unconditional love, support and sacrifice. Mom this book is for you.

Dad, **Ramchand Bahadur**, you have always been my best friend on levels that no daughter can ever comprehend, your continued love, though miles away, pushed me to complete this book.

My baby girl who complains I should have had another daughter so I do not have to worry about her, **Onalin**, I say thank you, for your kind words and smiles mixed with teenage shame.

My boys you are my life, every day I live for both of you, thank you **Milano** and **Alezandro**, for your unconditional companionship of innocence and love.

Neal, my best best best friend, soul-mate and husband, your continued support, drive and commitment to push me to finish this book is unwavering. I love you then, love you now, and will love you always. Like you said to me, if you had to choose a partner in your next life, you will chose me, because I allowed and supported you in your dream, I will surely choose you, because I know you would do the same for me.

BOOK FORMAT

The book was created for simple and pleasurable reading. It is very straightforward and thought provoking.

The book is designed in listings called rules. The rules or ways of thinking allow the reader to quickly identify and associate persona with the rule. The rules are also motivating as each rule encourages the reader to self-reflect at the end.

When the reader reads the book, the reader establishes a personal connection with the book, the book will draw the reader into its world of rules and ways of thinking, as the rules and ways of thinking are personal and talk to the reader in an intimate manner.

Enjoy Reading !!!!

TABLE OF CONTENTS

101 WAYS TO THINK LIKE A BUSINESS PERSON

1. I Am A Business Person
2. Dress For Your Business
3. Control Your Mind
4. Do Not Procrastinate
5. Follow Your Heart
6. Challenge Your Mind
7. Eat, Sleep and Breathe
8. I Am My Business
9. Cash Flow
10. Don't Be Afraid Of Money
11. Trust No One But Yourself
12. Be Positive
13. Focus! Focus! Focus!
14. Choose Your Network
15. Adding Value
16. Push Forward
17. Take Some Time For Yourself
18. Plan Your Days to Avoid Chaos
19. Educate Yourself About Your Industry
20. Don't Be A Doormat
21. Think Like a CEO, Act like a CEO
22. Ensure Your Customers Are Happy
23. Conflict Resolution - Key To Success
24. Customer Experience
25. Make Yourself Relevant
26. People Remember Constant
27. This Is All I Have
28. Make Yourself Known
29. Treat Others With Respect

30. Acknowledge Others - Say Thank You
31. Organise! Organise! Organise!
32. Be True And Real To Yourself
33. Swim with the Sharks
34. Delegate With Finesse
35. Have A Vision For Your Business
36. Be An Expert In Your Field
37. Knowing When To Say NO
38. Having Courage to Stand Up To Others
39. Trust Your Gut Feeling
40. Be Creative
41. Don't Be Afraid To Fail
42. Have Common Sense
43. Be A Quick Decision Maker
44. I Am A Risk Taker
45. Eliminate Inefficiency
46. Manage Your Time
47. Brainstorm
48. See The Big Picture
49. Having The Right Connections
50. Don't Overthink
51. Integrate, Correct, Prevent, Improve
52. Power of Positive Reinforcement
53. Failing to Plan is Planning to Fail
54. Safe Space
55. Narrow Your Inner Circle
56. Borrow A New Dimension
57. Think About Yourself
58. Project Plan It
59. Be Assertive Not Aggressive
60. Power of Positive Upward Posture
61. Earn Your Fortune By Working
62. Choose Your Networks
63. Take Care Of You

64. Be A Problem Solver
65. Believe In The Future
66. Think Outside Of The Box
67. Playground to Invest & Re-invest
68. Get Off The Complacency Boat
69. Professional, Purpose & Passion (3 P'S)
70. Fear - Your Biggest Obstacle
71. Put Your Thoughts On Paper
72. Don't Waste Time on Customers Who Don't Value Your Work
73. Manage Your Business, It Is Yours
74. Macro-Manage, not Micro-Manage
75. Be Results-Driven
76. Walk Away
77. People Believe What They See
78. Being Ruthless Is Good
79. Ask And You Shall Receive
80. Get Rid Of Them
81. Seek Out The Best Alignments
82. Be Money Conscious
83. Re-align Your Thoughts
84. The Plan
85. Opportunities For Improvement
86. Invest, Invest, Invest
87. Be Willing To Change
88. I Am The Breadwinner
89. Being Ready
90. Be Your Own Brand Ambassador
91. The Need
92. I Am The Driver
93. System And Process Everything
94. The Perfect Client
95. Customer's Pain
96. Assess The Competition

97. Have A Plan
98. Don't Give Up
99. Visualise Your Finish Line Daily
100. Your Social Responsibility
101. Dream, Never Stop Dreaming

101 WAYS TO THINK LIKE A BUSINESS PERSON

RULE # 1

I Am A Business Person

The basic and most important foundation of thinking like a business person is actually visualizing yourself as a business person. On most occasions you forget you are a business person with something to offer, that someone else wants. You are always so wrapped up in your multitasking, with your over-consuming, demanding life that you forget you are offering an intangible service or a tangible product for money, and you accept whatever your customers or clients want to pay you. You must not accept what customers feel they can pay you, you need to demand that they pay you for your value and the price you quoted for the job, service or product. Always remember you are a business person first, friend and family member after. Your business comes first and you are a business person.

SAY TO YOURSELF: I AM A BUSINESS PERSON AND SHOULD BE TREATED AS SUCH.

RULE # 2

Dress For Your Business

Very often the manner in which you dress dictates the way you feel, think and believe in yourself and value your self-worth. Your dress code sets the tone for the day. If you wear professional clothing related to your profession, you will feel confident, in control and feel as if you are ready to conquer the world. Even though you are categorized as a professional in your respective discipline or a consultant with a service to offer, and you are operating a home-based business, you need to remember to leave the t-shirts and sandals for the beach, the house-robes for the bedroom, the personal calls for break-time, and conduct your business work at home as if you were working for someone else, where the person in the office cubicle next to you is watching you constantly. To think like a business person you need to dress like a business person.

SAY TO YOURSELF: I DRESS LIKE A BUSINESS PERSON BECAUSE I AM A BUSINESS PERSON, I AM A RESPECTED PROFESSIONAL IN MY FIELD.

RULE # 3

Control Your Mind

Almost all the time, your mind plays games with you. You set out daily, with the best of intentions to be completely productive, and end the day totally wasted of useless non-money making, non-business tasks. The mind is often compared to a monkey swinging on a tree, just envision a monkey swinging from branch to branch, tree to tree for the entire day without stopping. All the monkey does is swing from branch to branch continuously, so too, your mind is racing with a million thoughts and scenarios, racing from branch to branch without a resting spot. If you control your mind, you can control your daily business actions and you can focus clearly on your daily business activities.

SAY TO YOURSELF: TODAY I WILL BEGIN TO CONTROL MY MIND.

RULE # 4

Do Not Procrastinate

Your biggest enemy is yourself. You have the tendency to put off your daily tasks as long you can, only because you can and are able to. You need set a realistic beginning date and an end date for the task, get the task completed and move on to the next task and so forth. Set achievable targets and reward yourself when targets have been achieved. Do not procrastinate. Get it done.

SAY TO YOURSELF: PROCRASTINATION IS MY ENEMY, I DO NOT WANT TO BE MY OWN ENEMY.

RULE # 5

Follow Your Heart

Following your heart is imperative and a must, as a business owner. A business owner who does not have his heart entwined and entangled in his business operations will soon have a failed business. Most business owners who follow their heart are passionate about what they are doing and are better able to make valuable business decisions. Having that innate burning passion inside of you will never lead you to defeat, for you will toil daily as a business owner to ensure your business' success. Managing a business without passion will soon leave you exhausted.

SAY TO YOURSELF: I AM PASSIONATE ABOUT MY BUSINESS.

RULE # 6

Challenge Your Mind

Challenge your mind outside the realm of your everyday thinking and thought processes. Think of different possibilities, and ways of doing tasks, push your thought processes to outside your boundaries and keep your mind active. A dormant or inactive mind will soon lead to your business demise. A business person always creates challenges, thereby breaking boundaries and creating new ones.

SAY TO YOURSELF: I COMMIT TO CHALLENGING MYSELF DAILY.

RULE # 7

Eat, Sleep and Breathe

You must eat, sleep, and breathe your business. This is a figurative term and not meant to be taken literally. However you need to understand the terminology as it relates to your business. Your business must become the essence of your being. All your waking and sleeping thoughts must be on your business. There must never be a downtime in a day when you stop thinking about your business. As you awake your first thoughts must be on how to make your business even more profitable, while you eat, your brain must be conditioned to think of your tasks ahead, and while you comfort yourself with sleep, your last thoughts before bed should be saying thank you to god for what you are blessed with and your business next steps.

SAY TO YOURSELF: I EAT, SLEEP, AND BREATHE MY BUSINESS DAILY, MY BUSINESS CONSUMES MY ENTIRE BEING.

RULE # 8

I Am My Business

You need to understand "your business is nothing without you". You need to condition your mind to accept that you are the foundation of your business, and without its foundation, the business will fall apart. You are your business, the success of your business depends on your acceptance of the phrase "I am my business".

SAY TO YOURSELF: I AM MY BUSINESS AND MY BUSINESS IS ME.

RULE # 9

Cash Flow

Pretty simple concept, even the youngest entrepreneur will tell you, without a cash-flow there is no business. Money needs to come into the business in the form of revenue (i.e. money obtained from sales minus operating expenses), and money needs to leave the business in the form of items purchased for the business. Maintaining a steady cash-flow is detrimental to the success of a business.

SAY TO YOURSELF: I AM ACCOUNTABLE FOR MY BUSINESS CASHFLOW.

RULE # 10

Don't Be Afraid Of Money

Far too many business owners are afraid of the mathematical aspects of money, its applications, its spreadsheets, its concepts and its terminologies. Don't be afraid of money, embrace it, understand it, love it, and become familiar with it. You do not need to be an expert on financials, however you need to demonstrate some level of financial understanding, that you are competent in managing the financial aspects of your business.

SAY TO YOURSELF: I WILL CHECK EVERY PENNY AND DOLLAR THAT COMES INTO MY BUSINESS.

RULE # 11

Trust No One But Yourself

The sooner you realize that there is no one else out there in the universe who will love and care for your business as much as you do, the sooner you will better be able to enjoy and grow your business. Trust no one except yourself, no one else has the interest of your business at heart as much as you do. Secretly, a lot of people will wish that you fail, as they are envious of your accomplishments and successes and will jump at every opportunity to demonstrate and support your failures rather than your successes.

SAY TO YOURSELF: I TRUST NO ONE BUT MYSELF, THE SUCCESS OF MY BUSINESS DEPENDS ON ME.

RULE # 12

Be Positive

As your business grows and establishes itself, you will soon realize your circle of friends would start to dwindle, shrink, and fall off one by one, and possibly disappear. Similar to a flower losing its petals one by one, you will be losing your friends one by one. Some friends may not understand why you are engrossed in your business and why you cannot afford the time to be away from the business, based on its operating structure. Other friends may despise you and your new found drive to achieve, and some may secretly wish you fail. Do not let the behavior from your circle of friends daunt you and bring you down and make you feel depressed. You have to keep a positive mentality and never take your eyes of the finish line. There will be days when you would want to give up, but keep on sowing the seeds of business growth and soon you will reap the fruits of your labour.

SAY TO YOURSELF: EACH DAY MY FINISH LINE IS GETTING CLOSER, I NEED NOT WORRY MYSELF OR SPARE THOUGHT TO MATTERS THAT DO NOT ADD VALUE TO MY BUSINESS AND MYSELF.

RULE # 13

Focus! Focus! Focus!

There are days your mind will work and there are days your mind will feel lazy, burnt out and exhausted. On some days you will feel completely out of energy, and your mood and personality will change, you will become agitated, angry, overwhelmed and extremely lost due to exhaustion and frustration. But you cannot give up or feel sorry for yourself, you need to divorce yourself from your environment, find a safe space, spend a few minutes re-evaluating your situation, and then approach your business with the ability to undertake one task at a time and see it until completion. Focus your mind and your thoughts on your business and its business growth, the more you hone your abilities to focus on your business tasks, the less likely you are to stray from your business, and less likely to create your own frustrations.

SAY TO YOURSELF: I WILL FOCUS! FOCUS! FOCUS! ON THE TASK AT HAND.

RULE # 14

Choose Your Network

The sooner you grasp the concept that a lot of these networking events are a waste of your valuable time and resources, the sooner you will be able to understand that you need to choose your networks wisely. Sadly many business owners have never quantified in dollars the billed cost to attend a networking event, be it a luncheon, a dinner or breakfast meeting. As a business owner we need to assign a dollar value (labour, transportation, attire, parking, stationery cost) for attending these workshops and assess its value to our business growth. Find that event that will bring you value. Define what value you anticipate to receive for attending that event and have a planned outcome before you attend that networking event. You need to attend the networking event you choose which will provide the most value to you. Not every networking that you are invited to, means you have to attend.

SAY TO YOURSELF: I NEED TO CHOOSE MY NETWORKS CAREFULLY. I WILL SENSIBLY NETWORK.

RULE # 15

Adding Value

Always ask yourself "Is the task I am doing today value added, meaning is this task adding value for my business and for me". If the task is not adding value then you should stop immediately and not proceed with the task. Each occasion you spend time on your business you should always ensure that the time spent is adding some sort of value for and value to your business. Wasting time on non-value added tasks diminishes your morale, and at the end of the day you still have a list of uncompleted tasks awaiting to be actioned.

SAY TO YOURSELF: EVERY TASK I DO MUST ADD VALUE TO MY BUSINESS. I WILL NOT WASTE TIME ON NON-VALUE ADDED TASKS.

RULE # 16

Push Forward

There are, and will be some days when you are beginning to second guess your business, its growth, its success or its ultimate failure. Not all days are the same, and not every day spent in the business is the same. Some days you feel perky and are ready to conquer the world, and other days you sit in your business, staring at the walls, questioning your abilities, while secretly hoping you get a walk in customer to increase your sales. You cannot allow yourself to be daunted by negative thoughts and feelings. You should just shrug it off, and keep pushing forward.

SAY TO YOURSELF: ON DAYS WHEN I DON'T FEEL FOR MY BUSINESS I HAVE TO PUSH FORWARD.

RULE # 17

Take Some Time For Yourself

Sometimes as a business person you will feel that you are riding waves, with lots of highs and lows. Your days will zip past you like a roller coaster, and you will wish you had more time in a day to complete your business related and personal tasks. At some point during this uproar and pandemonium you will become burnt out mentally and physically. You need to STOP and take some time out for yourself, to re-invigorate your soul, mind and thoughts. Divorce yourself from the pressures of your environment, take a walk outside, get some fresh air, but most importantly take some time for yourself.

SAY TO YOURSELF: TODAY I WILL TAKE SOME TIME OUT FOR MYSELF TO RE-ENERGISE MY SOUL.

RULE # 18

Plan Your Days to Avoid Chaos

The best and most successful business people always have their days planned properly. In advance, they know what they are doing, they know their appointments with their clients, and they have scheduled their own meetings weeks, so they become familiar with their planned activities. The main reason they schedule and plan every activity is to avoid chaos and confusion in their daily life, as they cannot afford chaos. Chaos breeds confusion and misunderstandings. Chaos and chaotic environments are costly mistakes when operating a business. These should be avoided at all costs.

SAY TO YOURSELF: I CANNOT AFFORD CHOAS, HENCE I WILL SCHEDULE AND PLAN MY DAYS. CHAOS IS COSTLY TO ME AS A BUSINESS PERSON.

RULE # 19

Educate Yourself About Your Industry

Most business owners are very learnt and knowledgeable about their industry. They are also self-educated as they take the time to read and learn about the industry within which they operate. The key to gaining knowledge and being successful is self-education and awareness in gathering information about industry changes, and being able to better adapt your business to the changes within the industry. As a business person you need to expand your mental horizon and capitalize on industry know-hows by staying informed and being informed.

SAY TO YOURSELF: I COMMITT TO EDUCATING MYSELF ABOUT MY INDUSTRY SO THAT I CAN BE ONE STEAP AHEAD ALWAYS.

RULE # 20

Don't Be A Doormat

A doormat, is a mat placed in front of a door where people stand on it and wipe their feet before they enter into the building. Sometimes running a business can be overwhelming and you succumb to the pressures of the business and become doormats for others to walk on. You forget how to negotiate business deals, you end up with the jobs under quoted. You struggle daily to find your place as a business person. As a business person you need to stand firm for your beliefs, quantify your worth, and demand the best from and out of your customers and employees. Do not be a doormat for others to trample and walk on.

SAY TO YOURSELF: I WILL NOT BE YOUR DOORMAT TO WALK ON.

RULE # 21

Think Like a CEO, Act like a CEO

It's all about your mindset. Your mind dictates the manner with which you carry out your daily business. If you are the owner and CEO of a business, you need to act like a CEO and an owner. You will only gain respect from your employees, customers and colleagues when you begin to think like a CEO. A CEO is a strategic planner, positioned at the helm of a business, just like the captain is the leader of his ship, and steers his ship away from tumultuous waters to calm waters, you also need to start staring your ship on the right course, away from torrents and under currents. Ask yourself, can I steer the ship on the right course if I assume the role of a worker? The answer is clearly no, so start thinking like a CEO, a strategic business planner and plan the path out for this business to travel.

SAY TO YOURSELF: I AM THE CEO. I WILL STOP THINKING LIKE A WORKER AND START THINKING LIKE THE CEO I AM.

RULE # 22

Ensure Your Customers Are Happy

Understand that your customers comes first, and without your customers you do not have a business. Always ensure your customers are happy and satisfied. Set your own benchmarks of satisfaction and ensure that you adhere to it when serving your customers. Resolve your customers problems as best as you can, customers love resolutions and finding solutions to their problems. Once you begin to show that you are definitely looking after your customer needs, you will immediately convert your customers from irate to happy customers and create an increase in your customer base. Go the extra mile to ensure your customers needs have been fulfilled. Happy customers means more referrals for you. Referrals for you means more business. More business is always good.

SAY TO YOURSELF: I NEED MY CUSTOMERS AS MUCH AS THEY NEED ME. MY CUSTOMERS SATISFACTION IS OF UTMOST PRIORITY TO ME.

RULE # 23

Conflict Resolution – Key To Success

As a business person, managing conflict is as paramount as ensuring your customers are satisfied. You will often encounter unpleasant circumstances where your employees will not adhere to your vision, mission and values, and where your customers will sometimes create unpleasant and uncomfortable situations to deal with. You need to learn the art of managing conflict, be able, ready and willing to diffuse an uncomfortable situation for the betterment of your business. Being able to manage uncomfortable situations is the key to managing conflict and resolving any probable or potential issues.

SAY TO YOURSELF: I WILL BEGIN TO UNDERSTAND THE ART OF MANAGING CONFLICT. KNOWING THIS IS KEY TO MAKING MY BUSINESS A SUCCESS.

RULE # 24

Customer Experience

This is a topic that I am most fond of speaking about, at business conferences and events. The customer experience, my experience and how as a business person I would like to be treated. As a business person, your sole purpose is to realize that without your customers, you can no longer remain in existence. You need to provide every customer with an experience. Providing a customer experience simply means each and every time a customer walks into your business place, or each and every time you meet with your customers, you are providing a particular experience you want your customers to remember. Once a customer walks into your business location, or initiates contact with your first line of defense, your customer service staff, you want to make sure that the impression provided is relevant, value added, pleasant and a reflection of your business values and goals. Every day, you continually need to self-assess and ask yourself if you are providing that customer experience. You need to constantly re-evaluate and ask yourself "if this is the experience I want my customers to have, and if it isn't, what is the experience I want my customers to have". I cannot over-emphasize how important having the right customer experience is to your business. You might have a million dollar customer walk into your business, a customer who is willing to pay for your service, and because of the experience provided to that customer, you will either loose that customer and all his contacts and referrals, or you would gain a customer who would freely refer you to his other business associates who may need your service or product. Always ensure you are providing the customer experience you would want when you walk into your own business. Always keep asking yourself what is the experience I want my customers to have and do I provide that experience for each of my customers? What do I want my customers to experience? What feelings do I want my customers to have? What do I want to ignite in my customers mind about my business?

SAY TO YOURSELF: MY CUSTOMERS SHOULD HAVE THE SAME EXPERIENCE EACH AND EVERY TIME, AN EXPERIENCE THAT INCITES THEM TO RETURN FOR MORE.

RULE # 25

Make Yourself Relevant

Most successful business persons strive and are successful because of being relevant. You need to make yourself relevant. You need to be able to keep up with the industry, be current and up-to-date with trends, statistics, needs, niches etc. You need to be able to ride the waves of success when they are flowing towards you and jump off the waves when you need to. Being relevant means being current and not being outdated. Being relevant means maximizing the use of technologies which makes your business efficient, current and up-to-date. Being relevant also means having a vested interest in the growth and success of your business.

SAY TO YOURSELF: BEING RELEVANT IS IMPORTANT AND DETRIMENTAL TO THE SUCCESS OF MY BUSINESS.

RULE # 26

People Remember Constant

Unfortunately you live in a world where technology is always changing and the world is progressing at a faster rate than is expected. Communications and communication techniques are forcing businesses to close its doors because they are not able to compete with technology and technological advances, however if you are constant in your business practices, and daily you are keeping up with the world and its advances your business will survive. Customers remember constant. Customers remember the same good service over and over, customers remember your above and beyond mentality to satisfy their needs. Staying constant allows you as a business person to thrive and succeed in a world of advancements, conglomerates, mergers, and business ventures.

SAY TO YOURSELF: PEOPLE REMEMBER CONSTANT, I

WILL REMIAN CONSTANT.

RULE # 27

This Is All I Have

Your thought is, to either make it or break it, meaning, you are managing your business to succeed or you are in it to fail. Every person who starts a business goes into the business with the intention to succeed. This is a good thought as long as you follow through with this thought. Often times, you become complacent and ignore the needs of the business. Also, you become overwhelmed by the demands of the business and give up, because the business is not structured and planned properly, therefore managing it becomes exhaustive. But if you are in it, to succeed, then all you need to tell yourself is, this is all I have and I have nothing else to fall back on. I have no other choice but to succeed because this is all I know. I am not skilled or versed in anything else, this is all I have and all I know. Once you have choices, you will be in your business with one leg in and one leg out, in this case you are not balanced and you will tumble over. If there is no choice, both legs will be positioned firmly in your business and you have a strong solid post and foundation to stand on.

SAY TO YOURSELF: THIS IS ALL I HAVE AND I DO NOT HAVE ANY OTHER OPTION BUT TO SUCCEED IN IT.

RULE # 28

Make Yourself Known

Make yourself known. Unknown people never get business deals, contracts and sales. You need to make your name and your brand like a staple in people's everyday conversation. The more people talk about you and your business the more visible your business becomes. Sometimes not every conversation about you may be a good business conversation, however it generates the business interest and buzz that you need. Making yourself known means that you need to be present, up and about, and networking like the tagline; here, there and everywhere. People do not buy services or products from the unknown, they buy from the known, because the known reputation, products and services has a story of its own to tell. Ensure that you have something unique about you that people will remember you by and you are known for it. When references are made, conversations are spoken about you or your product, your name will surface as the name and image to the reference.

SAY TO YOURSELF: I NEED TO BE KNOWN, UNKNOWN PEOPLE DO NOT GET BUSINESS.

RULE # 29

Treat Others With Respect

The sooner you realize that the world around you is fuelling your passion and your desire for your business, the sooner you will realize that you need every part of that world to help you run your business and make it a success. You need to accept that your business is not a sole entity but is inter-dependent on everything else. You need to have respect for, and a good working relationship with, your workers who work for you. You also need to understand that the delivery driver and the cleaner both play crucial roles to the success of your business. Once you conceptualize your business as an entity, reliant on others to sustain and support it, you will treat other parties with respect and love.

SAY TO YOURSELF: RESPECT FOR OTHERS IS VERY IMPORTANT.

RULE # 30

Acknowledge Others - Say Thank You

It is a good business skill to acknowledge others and say thank you. Even though you are the CEO of your business, there is no reason or harm in acknowledging others for their positive contributions to your business and simply saying thank you. It is very easy to reprimand an employee and point out their flaws and incompetency with tasks. As human beings you are often good at highlighting someone's wrong doing as it's a sign of strength to point out someone's flaws, however you need to move away and make a paradigm shift in mindset, that allows you commend, praise and support someone's strengths in your business. The more you praise and recognize a person's positive contributions to your success, the more the person and others around them are likely and willing to positively contribute to your success. After all, isn't this what you want, to be a success at your business, and have a successful business.

SAY TO YOURSELF: SAYING THANK YOU IS NOT THAT DIFFICULT.

RULE # 31

Organise! Organise! Organise!

Business people are generally very organized. Even though they thrive in chaos and love a hectic, fast paced environment to work in, they are always organized. They know their first steps they will take at the beginning of the day and they know their last steps at the end of the day. You need to organize your thoughts daily, revisit them in your head, and if they don't make sense throw them out. You need to be extremely organized, so much so that the processes flow mentally from your brain to real life actions. Daily your actions must be organized, so as to avoid any chaotic environments and situations, and if you do encounter a chaotic situation you are better able and positioned to deal with it, because your thoughts are streamlined and organized. You approach the chaos with an end result already in mind.

SAY TO YOURSELF: THE KEY TO MY SUCCESS IS ORGANISATION AND I WILL ORGANISE MYSELF FOR SUCCESS DAILY.

RULE # 32

Be True And Real To Yourself

Always be true to yourself. A real and true business person is always honest with themselves, and know what they are about (their limitations and their strengths). If you are not true to your heart and passion, you will not be successful. One of the best rules of running a business is being real and true to yourself. If your heart is not in it, your business you will fail. If you do not really explore your business possibilities you will fail. Being true to yourself, means you know when to quit and when to move forward with deals. Being true also means, if the business endeavor you may undertake is not feeling right inside, you will stop and rethink other possibilities. Always be true and real with yourself, your heart will never lead you astray, and you are the only person who will know if a deal or purchase is meant for you.

SAY TO YOURSELF: I WILL ALWAYS BE TRUE AND REAL TO MYSELF.

RULE # 33

Swim with the Sharks

Even though you are not a shark, or a big player in the business environment, this does not mean you cannot swim with sharks in shark infested waters. You need to learn the art of swimming with sharks, and not being afraid to deal with the sharks on a daily basis. The ocean is big enough for sharks and other fishes to co-exist. So to, the world is big enough for big businesses and small businesses to operate and co-exist. However, you need to be able to grow and sustain your business growth continuously, so that you are not consumed by bigger businesses. Sharks have a tendency to eat and digest less powerful fishes, similarly, big business have a tendency to consume less powerful, redundant and less applicable businesses in the market place.

SAY TO YOURSELF: I AM A GUPPY SWIMMING WITH SHARKS, HOWEVER WE CAN CO-EXIST IF I GROW AND SUSTAIN MY BUSINESS GROWTH.

RULE # 34

Delegate With Finesse

It is very important that you understand, you cannot do it all on your own, and that you need other skilled persons to work with you. You need to delegate your assigned business tasks to staff and employees you trust and have confidence in, that they will complete the assigned tasks within the specified time frame. Delegation is the key to your survival, delegate and manage accordingly. Hold staff accountable for delegated tasks and ensure results are achieved. Delegation simply means passing on tasks and job related duties to other staff members to ensure completion, while managing from above. Delegation also means being able to let go while placing your trust in others.

SAY TO YOURSELF: I WILL DELEGATE AND TRUST BECAUSE IT WORKS FOR MY BUSINESS CONTINUOUS GROWTH.

RULE # 35

Have A Vision For Your Business

A lot of times, most small business owners start up and open business because they have a particular skill and realize that this skill can make them wealthy, be an asset and an instrument of growth for them if they capitalize on it. Sadly most small business owners fail within the first three (3) years of operation, because they do not have a defined vision for their business. They are not able to formalize their thoughts onto paper and neglect focusing on long term growth and sustainability. Not having a vision means they do not have a direction with which to grow their business, neither do they have a defined growth pattern. They have not visualized the long term goal and growth of their business. A vision is like a map, it's a road map of your business, a guided tour of where you would like to visit and your destination stops along the way.

SAY TO YOURSELF: MY VISION IS MY ROADMAP FOR MY BUSINESS GROWTH AND SUSTAINABILITY.

RULE # 36

Be An Expert In Your Field

Always make sure that you are knowledgeable in your field of expertise. Be an expert in your field, learn, study, read, and expand your mental capacities. Knowledge is power, and having such a vast array of knowledge in your field is a very powerful tool and asset for you in the world of business. Assume the position of a sponge placed in water, just as a sponge soaks up all the water around it, so too a brain is thirsty for knowledge and will soak up all the knowledge around it. Having a vast array of knowledge and expertise will better assist you in carrying out your business and day to day business operations, transactions and negotiations.

SAY TO YOURSELF: I AM AN EXPERT IN MY FIELD BECAUSE I AM KNOWLEDGEABLE ABOUT MY FIELD.

RULE # 37

Knowing When To Say NO

A lot of times, as a business person you are often inundated with sales people, over bearing staff, business and business obligations. You feel like you are being pulled in a million directions all at once. It is an essential business skill to acquire the art of saying NO. Knowing when to say no, is an important skill. You will soon realize that not every sales person who is contact with you, needs your sale, and not every disgruntled employee needs ammunition to fuel their disgruntlement. Sometimes you just need to say enough is enough, and no to the request. It's an art to say NO, and not everyone is comfortable with it, however the guarantee is, the more times you say it, the more times you will get accustomed to saying it, and you will be better able to serve your business and its sustained growth on the right path.

SAY TO YOURSELF: SOMETIMES SAYING NO FEELS GOOD, I NEED TO SAY IT MORE OFTEN.

RULE # 38

Having Courage to Stand Up To Others

As you proceed through your business day, you would find out that people and situations will exhaust you. You will often feel that the entire world dynamics is against you, as if positioning you to fail at each endeavor. However you need to have the courage to stand up to others and fight for what you believe in, which is your mission and vision. You will need courage to challenge ideas put forth by other key team players in your business, sometimes you will need to stand up to everyone, even though you are the only one standing. Most importantly, you will need courage to make the best business decisions in the interest of your business, which sometimes others may not be too fond off.

SAY TO YOURSELF: I HAVE A FIRM BELIEF IN MYSLEF AND MY VALUES AND I HAVE THE COURAGE TO STAND UP TO OTHERS.

RULE # 39

Trust Your Gut Feeling

There is a feeling inside of us all, whereby, on most occasions we find ourselves saying, had I trusted my inner self thoughts I would have made the right decision. This is often called our gut feeling, and our gut feeling never leads us wrong. You need to trust that gut feeling inside of you when you are faced with a decision. Normally you are led by your mind and its thoughts, which pushes you to make logical decisions by thinking out the pros and cons of a situation, making the decision based on your analysis of the pros and cons. You need sometimes to forget logic, and trust your gut feeling inside of you, to make that decision. By trusting your gut feeling, you save yourself from making costly business decisions which could in-turn destroy your business growth.

SAY TO YOURSELF: I NEED TO TRUST MY GUT FEELING MORE, AS THIS INATE FEELING NEVER LEADS ME WRONG.

RULE # 40

Be Creative

A lot of us are very creative or have some aspect of creativity embedded within us, however we seldom tap into that creative pool which we are born with. As a business owner you need to tap into your creative inner being, stimulate your creative thought processes and let your creative juices flow, allowing you to bring creativity and adding a creative flare to your business. Make your business stand out by putting yourself out there to the universe, as a business with a personal touch, with some level of creativity, and you will be guaranteed customers, as customers like ingenuity and creativity with their service.

SAY TO YOURSELF: TODAY I AM BRINGING OUT MY CREATIVE FLARE TO MY BUSINESS.

RULE # 41

Don't Be Afraid To Fail

Our biggest obstacle in life is our mind preset and predetermined ability to fail, hence us suffering from the failure paradigm. Society has conditioned and brainwashed us into believing that failure is the ultimate doom and death of life. As a society we need to redefine and recondition our thinking of failure as not wrong, but rather a stepping stone to something better. So to, you need to understand that failing is sometimes good, as it gives you the ability to rethink, re-engineer, redesign your thoughts and actions into a more suitable and appropriate outcome. After all, you really didn't fail, you just did not achieve the desired outcome you set out to achieve. So what if you set another realistic outcome, definitely achievable and within reason, you would be able to achieve it now, then you would not have failed. The point here, is that failure or non-failure of a task is all dependent on the range and magnitude of the task assigned to be completed. Set reasonable tasks and you will not fail as your tasks will become achievable. Set unrealistic tasks and you will fail. Even failing with unrealistic tasks is good as you are better able to analyze and move forward understanding your shortcomings.

SAY TO YOURSELF: I AM NOT AFRAID TO FAIL, FAILING SOMETIMES IS A GOOD THING.

RULE # 42

Have Common Sense

As common as the words "common sense" are and is often used, it is not something that a lot of people actually have or possess. Common sense is often used as a colloquial word or dialect in everyday language in different countries around the world. It means being able to understand something without much thought put into it. Far too often most of us over think situations and scenarios causing confusion and sometimes our business demise in the end. Sometimes as a business person you need to be able to not overthink ideas, suggestions, or recommendations, you just need to understand its logic and thought process and be able to implement it. Having common sense is not often a common thing with most people, however it is an art that can be learnt and acquired, just by understanding the concept of de-simplifying your thoughts and processes and not making every task you encounter a difficult process.

SAY TO YOURSELF: I WILL MASTER THE ART OF HAVING COMMON SENSE.

RULE # 43

Be A Quick Decision Maker

Most wealthy business persons are extremely astute because they are able to make the best business decisions very quickly and on the spur of the moment. Some of the best and most effective decisions are made in the moment. Being a quick decision maker, means having the ability to think on the spur of the moment, the ability to make the most concise business oriented decision with the interest of your business at heart. In the world of business you feel like you have to make decisions every minute of the day. You need to be a master of decision making, you need to be able to make decisions on the spot for the betterment of your business. Your customers, depend on your ability to make a decision swift and quickly to close a sale or a business deal. Always have the best interest of your business in your heart and on your fingertips, so when called upon to make a business decision, you are better able to make a quick informed business decision.

SAY TO YOURSELF: I AM ABLE TO MAKE QUICK INFORMED BUSINESS DECISIONS IN THE INTEREST OF MY BUSINESS.

RULE # 44

I Am A Risk Taker

The old adage of "without risk there is no reward" is often true and applies to any business person undertaking a business venture. The fact that you have assumed the role of a business person means that you are willing to risk your current financial security for the unknown. Sadly, most of us do not realize that we are assuming the role of risk takers every minute of every day. We take risks every day, we risk our lives on the road during our daily commute, we risk consuming non-edible food, and sometimes we risk purchasing stocks and shares and investments to grow our financial portfolio. As a business person you have already taken the first step without realizing that you are a risk taker, so assume the role of a risk taker, capitalize on the risk, take calculated risk which will propel your business into the realm of successes. You need to understand that being in business is a risk. The fact that you decided to open a business is a risk, the fact that you invested money into a new business is a risk, and the fact that you base your livelihood on expecting customers to buy your product or service is a risk. You need to acknowledge that you are a risk taker and continue to take informed and calculated risks with your business to take it to the next level. After all you are in business to grow your business and make it successful.

SAY TO YOURSELF: I AM A RISK TAKER AND HAVE TAKEN RISK ALL MY LIFE. I WILL CONTINUE TO TAKE CALCULATED AND INFORMED BUSINESS RISK TO GROW MY BUSINESS.

RULE # 45

Eliminate Inefficiency

Far too often a business person's day is plagued with inefficiencies; from useless cold calls, to solving employee's problems, to fixing infrastructure and attending to non-value added tasks. One of the biggest reasons most businesses close its doors for good is its lack of being able to eliminate inefficiency. Very many have never quantified the cost to carry out the business in an efficient state versus the cost to carry out the business in its current inefficient state. Most business owners are just happy opening and closing their business and making money. As a business owner you need to eliminate inefficiencies as inefficiencies costs money, it is a waste of time and prolongs the inevitable. You need to understand that you may have inefficient processes, which can be streamlined to be more efficient, hence eliminating waste and ultimately extra costs. Creating efficiencies and structure in your business reduces the growth of inefficient processes. Eliminating inefficiency is good, you just need to understand how to do it, and applicable methods to use to get the job done.

SAY TO YOURSELF: I WILL WORK TO ELIMINATE INEFFICIENCY.

RULE # 46

Manage Your Time

Time is one of the most valuable resources in a business. Time can never be returned, time can never be quantified and there is a cost to time which most of us never notice. Every second and every minute, soon becomes the past, and past time cannot be recaptured neither can it be returned. Being a time juggler is as important as being a risk taker. Business persons often quantify and allocate a dollar value on time. The old saying; Time = Money (time equals money), is hugely important and relevant in conducting business operations, as wasting time means money is not being earned and the business is not growing. Time management is crucial in every aspect of life, including starting and growing a business. As a business owner, you need to realize the importance of your time, you need to understand that time wasted cannot be returned, but more importantly, there is a cost associated with your time. Your time has a value, it has an hourly rate and you should not allow your time to be wasted in non-paid hours, because you are losing time and money associated with non-payment. Not allocating time properly and wisely to your business will ultimately lead to its demise.

SAY TO YOURSELF: I SEE THE VALUE IN TIME = EQUALS MONEY AND I WILL DEVOTE MYSELF TO USING MY TIME IN THE WISEST POSSIBLE MANNER.

RULE # 47

Brainstorm

Brainstorming means the collective pitching of and notating on print, random ideas that populates into the mind, and making some sense out of these ideas. While brainstorming has always been in use and used, this concept is gaining tremendous appeal as more and more companies and organizations are placing enormous value on creative brainstorming or break-out sessions. Companies are seeing the value in and of brainstorming events, as creative juices are flowing from their employee's brains which could ultimately lead to better more efficient ways of doing tasks. Brainstorming is an excellent way of getting your ideas flowing, putting your thoughts on paper, even though they don't necessarily make sense at that point in time, these ideas are written on paper, so as to reflect and implement when necessary, in order to enhance your business operations. As a business owner it is better to utilize persons who have direct hands on experience with processes as they are the forefront process owners, and will have valuable insights during brainstorming sessions, assisting in elimination of waste and increasing efficiencies within your business processes.

SAY TO YOURSELF: BRAINSTORMING IS GOOD AND I WILL DEDICATE SOME TIME TO BRAINSTORMING EVERY DAY.

RULE # 48

See The Big Picture

Sometimes, the mind is often caught up in day to day details and trivialities, that you quickly loses your focus on your purpose and intended path. Very seldom do business owners ever expand their thoughts to think outside of the realm of their business. A lot of attention and focus is paid to small minute details, and more frequent than not, time and energy is spent on damage control of day to day issues. Sometimes business owners need to collate their thoughts and think in perspective, such that their thoughts are forward and outward thinking. Business owners need to think about the future, and not get caught up in the day to day running of the business operations. As a business owner, you should be able to take time off your schedule to look at the big picture, look at your business as if you are watching it from the outside, look at the big goals and the vision you had for your business, and ensure you are leading the business towards these goals and visions. As a business person you need to take a few minutes for yourself each day, re-calculate, re-focus, and re-energise yourself so that you are able to see the big picture and the real reason you are in business and works towards achieving your goal daily.

SAY TO YOURSELF: SEEING THE BIG PICTURE EVERYDAY ALLOWS ME TO FOCUS ON THE REAL REASON I AM IN BUSINESS.

RULE # 49

Having The Right Connections

Let's face it, in the business world and everyday life, nothing happens without connections. A business' success, almost if not in all cases depends on its interaction with other liked minded and non-liked minded minds. Only a naïve business person would assume that they can operate and thrive independent of the world around them. Business persons go out there and make themselves connected with the world, via all various types of networking. Business persons realize and understand inter-dependence in the business world. In order to be a success, business connections need to be established. Besides being established, connections should be right. Connections which are not right, sometimes becomes a burden, a heavy weight, and is very difficult to get rid of, as non-right connections bring negative energy into your business. Having the right connections and or contacts in the business world will either drive your business to be a success or be a struggle and a penultimate failure. Your level of success also depends on the type and quality of the connections you make. Established right connections, are able to open the right doors for you to grow your business along the intended path. Right connections make your business vision seem attainable, and relieves daily frustrations. As a business owner, you need to establish the right connections, connections that have a vested interest in your business and your success. Stay away from the wrong connections, as wrong connections feeds negative energy into your business and exhaust your time. You need to place yourself in strategic situations where there is benefit to you and your business. Your networking attempts should be strategic in nature. This approach is classified as "strategic networking", which means placing yourself in a favourable position to serve your goal.

SAY TO YOURSELF: I NEED TO ALIGN MYSELF WITH THE RIGHT CONNECTIONS.

RULE # 50

Don't Overthink

Sometimes the answers or solutions to the most difficult situations and circumstances can be found in the simplest of scenarios. Business owners spend a great deal of time in trying to analyze, rationalize, and find solutions to problems which are minute in detail and nature. The quickest resolve is to acknowledge the problem, find a short term and long term solution, apply the solution found to the problem and move on. Over-thinking leads to frustrations and unresolved problems. Solve the issue or problem and move on, there are many more problems and issues waiting to be solved and many more dollars waiting to be earned.

SAY TO YOURSELF: I WILL NOT OVERTHINK EVERYTHING. I WILL FIND SOLUTIONS QUICKLY AND EASILY.

RULE # 51

Integrate, Correct, Prevent, Improve

Part of the job of carrying on a successful business is being able to continuously apply the principles of integration, prevention, correction and improvement. These four (4) principles are interwoven and co-dependent on each other. As a person, you should be applying these to your daily life tasks in order to continually improve yourself, persona and personality, allowing you to grow and enhance your self being. When applied to business operations, as a business person, you need to continuously looks for areas of opportunity and improvements within your organization. You need to be constantly looking for ways to improve and to save money, to enhance your operations and maintain a cost effective business structure. You need to integrate business processes and process improvements within your business. You also need to ensure failed processes are corrected. Once corrected, you need to put measures in place to ensure that the process never fail again, that's called preventative action. Finally you need to ensure you are improving your operations daily.

SAY TO YOURSELF: I WILL CONTINUALLY UTILIZE PROCESS IMPROVEMENTS IN MY DAILY BUSINESS OPERATIONS.

RULE # 52

Power of Positive Reinforcement

If you want to generate more from your employees, you need to pay attention to the long-term advantage you gain from positive reinforcement. It is sometimes difficult to acknowledge and commend someone on their efforts, because we feel it is part of their job, so they do not need to be thanked for doing a job they are already being paid to do. However, the power of positive reinforcement is tremendous and the gains are multitude, converting into profit for you. Positive reinforcement makes an employee feel happy, it also lifts the self-esteem of the employee, allowing them to feel valued and worthy. As a business owner, you need to seek out opportunities for positive conversations with your employees, enable them to produce more and commend them when they do. After all, everyone enjoys a compliment.

SAY TO YOURSELF: I NEED TO SEEK OUT THE POSITIVE AND REINFORCE IT.

RULE # 53

Failing to Plan is Planning to Fail

Every task undertaken in life should generally be planned. Tasks normally have a beginning, a middle and an end. Following that planning format, tasks are normally completed within a specified timeframe, with achievable results, and with most parties being satisfied. When applied to your business, similar process should be followed. In business every task should be looked at as a process. If the process is not followed, then failure to achieve will dominate. As you begin your work processes, and you have failed to plan in advance, expect that you have set yourself up for failure.

SAY TO YOURSELF: I WILL PLAN, AND NOT FAIL TO PLAN.

RULE # 54

Safe Space

If you want your employees to succeed and excel with the work that they are hired to do, you need to create at safe space for them. You can also create that safe space for yourself. A safe space, is a place where employees feel they are most comfortable, most trusted and most likely will not want to leave. Generally, employees believe they own their cubicle or desk or office, or whatever part of the company they perform their work in. Once the employees begin to feel comfortable in that space, it becomes their safe space. Having a safe space for employees, transcend into happy, productive employees. As a business owner you need to create a safe space for your employees. If you value your employees, and the worth that each person brings forth, you will ensure your employees are happy and contented, and in return, it is guaranteed you will have productive employees.

SAY TO YOURSELF: I WILL CREATE SAFE SPACES FOR MY EMPLOYEES.

RULE # 55

Narrow Your Inner Circle

A business person circle of friends, acquaintances, business colleagues, associates and employees are normally quite large. The circle becomes large over a period of time, by the acquisition of deals, contracts, and business services. Most times, people in this circle are one-off acquaintances, and are not needed further than the required time of meeting. Most successful business people, keep their inner circle of friends, small and minute. These are the colleagues that they can depend on, when in need. Having a huge circle of colleagues and friends does not add any more value than a smaller circle of friends. Know your colleagues in-detail, and keep your inner circle small. Small inner circles are reliable, dependent, and always available.

SAY TO YOURSELF: I WILL KEEP MY INNER CIRCLE SMALL.

RULE # 56

Borrow A New Dimension

Most of the non-business people are dimensional thinkers, they think within a certain framework, see things as being either black or white, possibly some shades of grey. They hold on to certain ways or methods of doing things, and are sometimes uncomfortable when a new method or approach is offered up as an alternate to an existing situation. As a business person, you need to be able to experience that level of comfort which allows you to borrow a new dimension, and visualize your tasks in a new dimensional realm. New dimensions or new methods of viewing the same old item, isn't a bad idea, and can possibly eliminate wastage and other extra costs associated with doing a task, a set specific way. You need to borrow that new dimension, test it out, play with it, and allow yourself as a business person to explore other possibilities.

SAY TO YOURSELF: I WILL BORROW NEW DIMENSIONS TO ENHANCE MY UNDERSTANDING OF LOOKING AT A NEW METHOD OF DOING AN OLD TASK.

RULE # 57

Think About Yourself

Being a business person can become overwhelming on some days, and on other days you may wish you had a full time 8am - 4pm type of job. You have to always remember, you are in business for yourself, you are being a business person for yourself, because you want to and you delight in working flexible hours, with a huge rush of adrenaline within you, pumping blood feverishly throughout your body, and giving you the zeal to move forward every day. As a business person, against all the heartaches that come with carrying on a business, added on to the lack of time, you would rather be working for yourself, following your passion, allowing your creative juices to flow, on your own time, rather than working for someone else, who makes you unhappy internally. Think about yourself every day, think about what makes you click daily, what drives you to get up every day more enthusiastic than the day before, what challenges you, and what you require from life. Be SELFISH and think about yourself, your needs, your dreams, your goals and your ambitions.

SAY TO YOURSELF: I WILL BE SELFISH AND THINK ABOUT MYSELF EVERYDAY.

RULE # 58

Project Plan It

Project plan it, this is a favorite phrase used in the consulting and manufacturing industry. This phrase can be applied to the all aspects of life and business. In every aspect of running and managing a business you need to plan and strategize your next move, so to in every aspect of planning you need to put a time frame to meeting your achievable requirements. Simply put this means that you need to look at all tasks as projects, either as a small project, a medium project or a large project. Once you define that you have a project to be worked on, you then decide the time frame within which you would like to complete the project and assign specific timelines to tasks identified in the project. There are numerous software and computer applications available in the market place, which makes it very easy and simple to plan projects and conduct follow ups with projects, to ensure completion to specified timelines. Project planning is an awesome tool to use, and as a business person, you need to embrace this tool, and use it to the best of your ability, as it will make managing and completing your tasks simpler and easier.

SAY TO YOURSELF: I LOOK AT ALL TASKS AS PROJECTS.

RULE # 59

Be Assertive Not Aggressive

Assertiveness and aggressiveness are sometimes used interchangeably in the business world as a definition of a person's character. This should not be, as both words have its own meaning and the differences are quite distinct. Aggressive is associated with a type of behavior or behavior trait that is rough around the edges, tough to deal with, and sometimes scary as intentional conflict emerges. Assertive means being bold, daring and persistent. Being assertive means communicating your message with a command of authority and confidence, however not crossing the lines of aggressive where contact is involved. As a business owner you should adopt the attitude of being assertive but not aggressive in order to propel yourself and make yourself known in the world of business. Being assertive speaks to your style, that you know what you are doing and you know how to achieve what you set your mind to.

SAY TO YOURSELF: I AM ASSERTIVE.

RULE # 60

Power of Positive Upward Posture

For many, many years, ancient philosophers, gurus, teachers and people in general have understood the philosophy of positive upward posture. Simply put, the more erect and upward your body posture, the more air and energy flows into and out of your body, causing your blood to circulate at a faster rate, getting rid of impurities in the blood as it circulates. The power of positive upward posture is not to be taken lightly, as erect and upward posture generates positive ions in the blood, negative slouching posture, puts tension on the muscles and body, forcing slowdown of blood flow, thereby keeping impurities in the blood and body. As a business owner, you need to grasp the ancient concept as it has been tried, is true and has been accepted. Accept that positive upward posture can work for you, enhance your thought processes and increase your levels of adrenaline in the body and blood, thereby allowing you to push forward in your business against all physical setbacks from your body.

SAY TO YOURSELF: I NEED TO MAINTAIN GOOD POSTURE.

RULE # 61

Earn Your Fortune By Working

Unless you are "born with a gold spoon", which means you are born into wealth, wealth follows you around, and money accumulation is not problem, then most likely you have to earn your fortune by working. Earning your fortune by working is a pretty simply concept, it just means that you apply yourself diligently to any money related task ensuring your goal is attainable. Earn your fortune by working also means that you must have enough self-discipline to condition your mind to think, do and act as a business person at all times. As a business person you also need to see your business as work, and not a place to socialize and waste time. Always remember, work brings money, money means income, income translates into revenue, which propels your business to another level.

SAY TO YOURSELF: I WILL APPLY MYSELF DILIGENTLY TO MY BUSINESS.

RULE # 62

Choose Your Networks

A lots of business failures occur because the businesses are established within the wrong networks and niches. A business will never survive if its customer base is not affiliated with the right network and right niche. Niches were established as specific communities within which a business can function and survive while providing a service or product. If the product or service is of no use or non-essential to that niche or network, then the product will soon have a timely death. As a business owner you need choose your network correctly, put some thought into the type of customers you would want for your business as well as the amount of money you would like each customer to spend in your business.

Create and establish your networks, and build your own niches, to grow your business successfully.

SAY TO YOURSELF: I WILL CHOOSE MY NETWORKS CORRECTLY.

RULE # 63

Take Care Of You

A lot of times, you are caught up in the day to day business operations, day to day life scenarios and day to day emergencies which pop up throughout the day. These "life happens" scenarios, totally mess up your psyche, remove your focus from your business, and throw your life into a whirlwind of unpredictables. It often seems like you cannot cope anymore and life has been one obstacle after another. You need to take care of you. You need to make sure you are happy. You need to realize you come first. If you cannot take care of you then you cannot take care of others, let alone your business. You are of no benefit to others if you are not who you truly aspire to be. As a business person you need to take care of you before you can take care of your business. You need to realize you are no good to your business, rather you become toxic to your business and the business environment, if you have not taken care of yourself.

SAY TO YOURSELF: TODAY I AM TAKING CARE OF ME.

RULE # 64

Be A Problem Solver

Problems emerge constantly in business, problems that can be rectified immediately, called short term problems, or problems which needs a period of time to be resolved, most likely involving some type of change, these are called long term problems. Either way, problems do exist and will continue to exist in any business. The key to resolution is to be a problem solver. Acknowledge the problem, and provide a remedy either in the short term to close the problem for a little while, or long term to close the matter completely. As a business owner, you need to wear a problem solver hat daily, diagnose problems, provide solutions and move on. The longer the problems exist, the more infestive and delay-tensive matters remain open. Solve problems and move on, there is money to be made, no time to waste on problems that do not generate money.

SAY TO YOURSELF: I AM A PROBLEM SOLVER.

RULE # 65

Believe In The Future

Once you realize that you cannot return to the past, neither can you change the past, you will begin believing in the future. It takes a lot of faith, strength and discipline to believe in the future, as many times, you tend to hold on to the past, its accomplishments and failures. Many times you tend to not want to let go of the past, as you may feel it is the only thing or moment you have in this life. However, you need to step away physically and mentally from this world, observe yourself from the outside, and take a closer look at what you have accomplished, what you have failed at and what you need to accomplish. Once you have visualized what you desire and how you can accomplish it, you then need to believe in the future and believe that, what you desire is achievable. Learn from past mistakes, past is gone never to be returned, so learn from it, and move on to bigger brighter dreams and possibilities. As a business owner you need to do exactly the same thing, accept the past, devoid yourself from the past, acknowledge your failed goals and successes and apply future visions to your business and future.

SAY TO YOURSELF: THE FUTURE IS ALL I HAVE.

RULE # 66

Think Outside Of The Box

In this life you live, you have always forced on yourself limits and boundaries. You have forced yourself to live within a box-typed environment that you have created. In order to exist and sustain yourself, you live within the realm of your self-imposed boundaries and restrictions. You are able to achieve your potential and goals set. However, you have not realized your true potential, and never will, unless you remove yourself from your boxed-in environment and think outside the box, think of the possibilities and progress, possibilities of making money and making a profit. As a business person, do not box-in your thought processes, allow your mind to flow freely, allow your mind to believe in possibilities, and find creative solutions and avenues to grow your business. Think outside the box and enjoy the profits that await you.

SAY TO YOURSELF: I AM WIDENING MY MIND TO THINK OUTSIDE THE BOX.

RULE # 67

Playground to Invest & Re-invest

Don't be afraid or intimidated by the stock market, the frequency, the numbers and its transactions. Often it is said, the stock market is a "big boy's" playground, a place where "big boys" communicate, dance, play, trade, take risk, laugh, smile, throw tantrums and celebrate. This playground should not be run by "big boys" only, in this modern age, it has become a level playing field where traders are both male and female, the only distinguishing characteristic between male and female traders, is the age old concept of "money". The market does not care if you are male or female, black, white or green, born in east, west, north or south, live in a hut or a mansion, ride a bicycle or drive a Ferrari, all the market cares about is your money and your ability to make sensible investment decisions. Your investment decisions could be long term or short term, and made in the best interest of your business and personal goals. As a business person, you should be able to invest and re-invest your money, make sensible money decisions, recuperate profits and interests, and never be afraid of the market. Always keep yourself informed of the market. Read! Read! Read!

SAY TO YOURSELF: I LIKE STOCKS AND TRADES, IT'S MY PLAYGROUND.

RULE # 68

Get Off The Complacency Boat

The sooner you realize that you need to get off the complacency boat and ride the wave of progress and processes, you will better be able to understand life and money. Understanding that money open doors, that money makes you happy, that money eliminates poverty, money converts needs into wants and that money makes you smile, then you can understand the value of money and the need to accumulate and work for money in such a haste that you do not have time for non-value money related associations and tasks. Once you understand that money solves problems, and money becomes a necessity in life, you will no longer accept complacency and you will begin to respect, that which gives you life and gives you a sense of fulfilment. As a business owner you need to accept that money is the foundation of your business, without it, your business existence is short lived, your business doors will close and your employees will be without an income. Stop making excuses for yourself, stop being complacent and get off the complacency boat, as you do not belong on that boat if you are a business owner.

SAY TO YOURSELF: I AM NOT GOING TO BE COMPLACENT.

RULE # 69

The 3 P's

Professional, Purpose & Passion

In the world of Marketing, reference is always made to the 4P's, which are Price, Product, Place, Promotion. When I reference, in this book, the 3P's, it is referenced to what I believe as the most important business characteristics or traits to have; Professionalism, Purpose and Passion. Being professional and upholding professionalism, finding your purpose, and living life with passion. Being professional and upholding professionalism is one of the underlying facets of being in business. Professionalism is a given in any business transaction you undertake. Quite often as a business person you are judged by your behavior and the manner in which you carry out yourself. Sometimes when you least expect it, people are associating you with your business, they recognize you, they know you, you are becoming known. Most frequently this occurs on your own personal time, in flights, in the coffee shop or even in the grocery. Always maintain yourself with professionalism and in a professional manner as the world is watching you at all times.

Finding your purpose seems like a long, long road, a road without any end. It becomes frustrating, tiring and exhausting when you cannot find your purpose and understand what your life was meant to be and why you are placed on this earth. Finding your purpose takes time, but once found, life becomes very enjoyable and achievable. As a business owner, once you find your purpose and find out the real reason you are in business, you are better able to take the business and make it a success.

Living life with passion is never exhausting, neither is it lost and empty. Life with passion is filled with joy and happiness, as you become so passionate about life that you use it wisely, you value your time and enjoy living every day. Passion becomes your reason for living, passion enhances your purpose and passion transcends into your professional life. As a business person, you must be passionate about your business, that you are determined to succeed all the time. Not just determined to succeed but determined to make every facet of your business a success.

SAY TO YOURSELF: I WILL PRACTICE THE 3 P'S.

RULE # 70

Fear - Your Biggest Obstacle

Your biggest obstacle in life is fear. Fear keeps you from achieving your true potential, fear disables your mind from the world, fear breaks you as a person, fear stops you from moving forward in life. Fear is definitely your biggest obstacle in life. As humans, you are afraid of failure, so you become paralyzed by your fear of failure that you never get to experience your true potential and realize who you could become in this life. As a business person, you need to let go of your fear of the world of business, let go of any fears that are holding you back, and move forward with your business. As a business person living in fear of failure, you force yourself to settle for mediocrity, and you allow mediocre work to become the norm. Let go of the fear holding you down from succeeding and soar high above the clouds, take your business to the place it belongs, on top of the world.

SAY TO YOURSELF: I NO LONGER HAVE FEAR.

RULE # 71

Put Your Thoughts On Paper

Most of the best ideas are kept in the mind. These ideas sometimes die with the owners. Lovely creative ideas never get to be born to fruition, since the owners of these ideas constantly store these ideas in the "mind-bank". As a person and a business owner, you need to start putting your thoughts on paper. The saying of "seeing is believing", or "visualizing becomes reality" is very true, as once these ideas are on paper, you can revisit the ideas daily and frequently, you can hone and massage your ideas, add or delete as needed until your idea become tangible and real. As a business owner you need to take the first step to making your business real, you need to put your thoughts on paper. Sit and stare at your thoughts because the thoughts are yours, and they are as real as you would like it to be.

SAY TO YOURSELF: TODAY MY THOUGHTS ARE WRITTEN ON PAPER.

RULE # 72

Don't Waste Time on Customers Who Don't Value Your Work

Don't waste time and energy on customers who don't value your work. If they don't value your work, they will never value your time. Customers always want something for nothing. Customers will come to you requiring your product or service, however they come to your business with the mindset that they will pay the price they want, not the price that you have requested of them. Customers who undervalue your work, and do not want to pay for your product or service, are not worth your time and effort. It is better to walk away from a customer who refuses to acknowledge your work and value, than to provide your product or service at a lower reduced price, as in both cases you have undersold yourself and are operating at a loss rather than a profit or break even position. As a business owner, stand firm, believe in your product or service, and never ever let any of your customers set a value and price for your work. Saying no is better than working for free.

SAY TO YOURSELF: I AM NOT WASTING TIME ON FALSE CUSTOMERS.

RULE # 73

Manage Your Business, It Is Yours

Every aspect of a business must be managed daily, from the receptionist who greets persons, to the delivery guy delivering your products, to the janitorial staff and executive management. The receptionist provides the first impression to anyone walking into your business, if your receptionist persona screams disorganization and unprofessionalism, most likely your business is a reflection of your main line person. So to, if your delivery driver, delivering your products, does not take pride in the delivery aspect, the delivery driver is conveying an image to your customers, which says you lack pride in what you stand for and believe in. As a business owner you need to manage your business in the manner which you require and ensure that your staff recruited are a reflection of you, your goals and your vision. If your staff do not reflect your values, they will not be adding to your business, neither will they provide any value to your business growth. Sadly, you need to get rid of the staff who are not aligned with your core values and employ staff willing to adopt your core values, and ride the high tide with you to success. If you are successful, your staff will also reap your success.

SAY TO YOURSELF: THIS IS MY BUSINESS, I WILL MANAGE IT MY WAY

RULE # 74

Macro-Manage, not Micro-Manage

Being a manager is quite tricky, as you are dealing with different personalities, different levels of belonging, dedication and commitment. Some of your staff are working because your business is a stepping stone to their career dreams, some are working because they need the money, and other are working for you because they have a vested interest in seeing you succeed. Whatever reason your staff works for you, you need to learn the art of macro-managing rather than micro-managing. Micro-managing breaks your staff morale, limits their creativity, makes them complacent, and you will have a high turnover, plenty of hours training and cross training staff to fill in replacements. A micro-manager, is involved in the day to day managing of every single and specific aspect of the business and staff tasks. Micro-managers needs to be involved in every task, to feel needed and wanted. Micro-managing is bad, there is never any good that can emerge from having your hands in every aspect of your business. Macro-managers are the best type of managers, as they allow their employees to be creative, and prove themselves, they allow their employees to set their goals as high as they want, Employees working with macro-managers always have something to prove to themselves and will work to achieve it. Micro-managers cost your business loss revenue, macro-managers have the ability to bring out the best in an employee, hence the bottom line is always increased as employees working for macro-managers are always looking and seeking for better ways to improve and reduce costs. As a business owner, you need to be a macro-manager and allow your employees to prove their worth, give them enough space to succeed, however tighten the reins when needed. Your employees will love you for it.

SAY TO YOURSELF: I AM A MACRO-MANAGER

RULE # 75

Be Results-Driven

Adopting the results-driven path, takes your business to a whole new different level. As you become more results-driven and results-focused, you will notice you have less wastage, more allocated resources and you are more goal focused. Being results-driven allows you as a business owner to quantify and highlight tasks which need to be achieved and you can now decide methods in which you can achieve your tasks. The more you are able to itemize your tasks and achieve it, the more results-driven you become, as you now have an attainable target to achieve. All business owners strive to have attainable targets, however this is not an easy goal, as you need to focus, hone in on your thoughts and dictate your tasks to paper. Once you begin to see results, you are better able to itemize tasks, achieve it and continue on your results-driven path. As a business owner, create that results driven path for yourself, make your goals attainable and achievable.

SAY TO YOURSELF: I WILL CREATE MY RESULTS DRIVEN PATH.

RULE # 76

Walk Away

Sometimes, some types of business deals we get into are not always in our best interest, takes too much time, becomes exhaustive and not worth the money in the end. Some business people have ill-fated intentions, and may not have your best interest at heart. You need to be able to stand firm, and walk away from a business deal if you feel uncomfortable. You need to assess and reassess the situation, look at the pros and cons, and mentally condition your mind to walk away, without pondering and wasting another second of your time, wondering if the decision you made is right or wrong.

SAY TO YOURSELF: ONE, TWO, THREE, I AM WALKING AWAY.

RULE # 77

People Believe What They See

In most cases and scenarios in life, people are judged by their appearance and physical attributes. Sometimes appearances do not reflect a person's true abilities, however it is often used as a measure of a person competencies and abilities. Physical attributes and limitations should never be used as a measure of a person abilities. However, and as unfortunate as it is, physical attributes and appearances dictate the type, quantity and dollar value of the business acquisitions and deals you will secure. As a business owner, you need to walk with your head held high, with a certain degree of confidence, as if the world is your playground and you came out to play. You can play with an empty bank account, but the world doesn't need to know your bank account is empty. People believe what they see, and what you want your customers to see is a very confident, in control, successful business person.

SAY TO YOURSELF: WATCH ME NOW, I AM IN CONTROL, CONFIDENT AND SUCCESSFUL.

RULE # 78

Being Ruthless Is Good

In the world of business being ruthless always seems like a bad act, seems like a tyrant is taking over, and like the leader is self-serving. In most cases, ruthlessness is synonymous with success in business, as it's a self-defining, selfish acquisition of power. Being ruthless is acceptable and is a good thing in the business world. Most business leaders are ruthless in making the best decisions in the interest of their company. No leader in business wants to fail, failure is not an option, hence coining the terminology ruthlessness and equating it to business success. As a business leader, you need to be ruthless to the extent that you gain your customer's trust and respect. As a business leader you also want to know that your customers are aligning with you because of who you are as a business person, what you believe and what you stand for. You cannot grow your business and be a success if you are kind hearted and generous, you might as well open a walk-in, free for all charity and forget you own a business, Your goal is to make a profit and be self-sustaining. You need to be ruthless and make business decisions in the best interest of the company.

SAY TO YOURSELF: I NEED TO BE RUTHLESS FOR THE BENEFIT OF MY BUSINESS.

RULE # 79

Ask And You Shall Receive

Philosophers, coaches, speakers and leaders are always asking. If ever you have time, observe their actions and study their persona and you will notice that the universe is their playground. Their playground is big, it's huge, it's massive and there are no boundaries to hold them in. These great minds and thinkers are forward thinking. After studying their thought processes and actions, you will notice that each one of them lives by the philosophy of "asking and you shall receive". As a business person, you need to put it out there to the universe what you require, spell it out to the universe as if the universe is understanding and accepting of you and granting your requests. Ask the universe for money, for successful paths, for a desire to succeed and let the universe unfold your dreams within your reach and your eyes. If you ask the universe for small favors, small quantifiable amounts, it will repay you in small favors and quantifiable amounts, if you ask in big increments, be prepared to have and accept your requests paid in big increments. Ask big and the universe will pay you big. Don't be afraid to ask.

SAY TO YOURSELF: I AM NOT AFRAID TO ASK.

RULE # 80

Get Rid Of Them

It's a waste of time, effort and money to trail and carry employees who are non-contributing to your success and your business success. These employees are dead weight and are non-value added to your business. Sometimes, these non-contributing employees are more interested in the paycheck at the end of the week or pay cycle, and are considered as "counting hours employees". As a business person you need to get rid of these employees, in the most legal manner of course, avoiding possible litigation, but get rid of them, they are sometimes synonymous to leeches on animals, or fleas on dogs, they will suck the last once of sanity from you, make you waste countless hours attending to their wasted demands, and mentally tire and exhaust you. If your employees do not have your business vision and goals at heart, it is very safe to say that they do not belong in your business and have no interest in working with you. You need to get rid of them, and recruit the best who will carry forth your vision and mission and ensure you are a success and your business is a success.

SAY TO YOURSELF: TODAY I WILL "CLEAN HOUSE" AND GET RID OF NON-VALUE ADDING EMPLOYEES.

RULE # 81

Seek Out The Best Alignments

The business world is made up of newbies, existing and super-successfuls. The newbies are those newcomers who are establishing themselves as legitimate businesses and building credibility in the marketplace. The existing are considered as already established businesses, been through the teething process and are growing at a steady pace. The super-successfuls, are those who have the "been there done that" mentality, they have experienced the best of the best, the worst of the worst, survived it all, grew exponentially and are at a stage where growth and success are the only two possible outcomes. As a business person, regardless of the size and years in business, you need to align yourself with business partners who share similar interests and can steer you and your business in the right path. These business partners that you align yourself with, will most likely, more often than any other business partner, provide the most valuable business advice in terms of growth and stability. Choose wisely and align with those who will provide the best business advice to you, and those who delight in your successes.

SAY TO YOURSELF: I WILL CHOOSE WISELY TO ALIGN MYSELF

RULE # 82

Be Money Conscious

From a simple survey of 100 persons, no specific ethnicity, gender, class or age, almost 85% of the survey had no idea of their financial status or financial standing. Most interviewed were afraid of financials, and not interested in money as an entity, but rather interested in money as a resource to purchase consumables. In the business world, if this everyday theory is applied, which identifies most people generally being afraid of money and are not money conscious, as businesses and business owners, the businesses are set to fail from the beginning. As a business owner, you need to understand your financials, you need to understand your money, your purchases, your expenses, your revenue received, your sales and every aspect of your business pertaining to money. Furthermore as a business owner you need to fully grasp the concept that without money, your business will fail immediately as there are no grounds for the business to sustain itself. As a business owner you need to be extremely money conscious, you need to ensure every day you are speaking the financial lingo of money, balancing your financial transactions, and that you are treating your money as an asset the same way you would treat your vehicle. Being money conscious will save you from unforeseen circumstances and possible failures.

SAY TO YOURSELF: I WILL BE MORE CONSCIOUS ABOUT MONEY AND MY BUSINESS.

RULE # 83

Re-align Your Thoughts

Sometimes in the midst of success there are possible roadblocks, some failures and obstacles which may occur. Most times the path to success is laden with roses, and it's an easy walk once the path is found. However, in the midst of success, obstacles lie, unforeseen obstacles which are placed there to propel you to a new path and new way of thinking. As a business person, you need to recognize the failing paths and re-organize yourself for success. You need to re-align your thoughts for success and remove the unsuccessful endeavors from your to-do lists. As a business person you need to concentrate your efforts on tasks which generates money, and allow for the obstacles and negativity surrounding you to fall off the bandwagon, as you thread through the obstacle path on your way to the path that brings you least resistance and success.

SAY TO YOURSELF: I NEED TO FIND MY PATHS FOR SUCCESS.

RULE # 84

The Plan

It is safe to say that every small business owner, entrepreneur, business person, or any person who dabbled in business had a great idea at one point in time. After all, great ideas make great businesses. Let's rephrase, great ideas make great business if they are fully actioned and implemented. As a business owner, you become overwhelmed with business ideas, business plans, business thoughts and money making ideas. Guaranteed, almost 95% of your ideas are never implemented, because you are busy chasing the next great idea in your head. You did not have time to finish the first thought process furthermore the implementation process for your existing idea and you are on to the next. As a business person you need to visualize your initial idea, convert your idea into a plan, implement your plan, and take specific decisive decisions to grow your idea and business into a success. Once that idea has been completed, you can move along to the next big idea in your head and bring it to fruition and implementation, ensuring success of every idea.

SAY TO YOURSELF: I KNOW THE PLAN, I HAVE THE PLAN.

RULE # 85

Opportunities For Improvement

In every part life there are always opportunities for improvements and making life better and more enjoyable. Similarly, in every aspect of business there are opportunities for improvement, opportunities for business growth, to enhance processes, to supersede customer expectations and to deliver exceptional results repeatedly. As a business person, your mindset needs to be keen and sharp, so that you are able to grasp and identify these opportunities for improvement, and take advantage of it as it unfolds. You need to be able to examine all aspects of your business in a detailed manner, identify opportunities for improvement and initiate implementation plans, to capitalize on these opportunities for improvements. Don't let these opportunities pass you by, as they seldom ever return.

SAY TO YOURSELF: I CAN'T LET THESE OPPORTUNITIES PASS ME BY.

RULE # 86

Invest, Invest, Invest

Smart business people are always looking for ways and means of investing their money, so that they can acquire additional monies to carry out their business goals. Part of running a successful and sustainable business is investing. Investing allows your money to double, triple and sometimes quadruple in value. As a business person you have to decide if you are risk aversive or enjoy risk. If you are a smart investor, you would normally invest in low risk items to ensure that at the end of the investment timeframe, you have your monies back (principal) plus additional monies paid out to you (interest). If you enjoy risk, you would invest in high risk options, with quick yields, paying close attention to your money, and knowing when to close an investment and walk away with your money in hand plus interest. Some business owners like medium risk, a little bit of excitement watching their money grow, however these are calculated investors, who enjoy the thrill, but are risk aversive at the same time. Regardless of what type of investor you are, it is wise to invest some of your monies, as the returns on investment becomes a good injection of monies into your business to expand and catapult it further.

SAY TO YOURSELF: I WILL INVEST, I NEED TO INVEST.

RULE # 87

Be Willing To Change

Change is the only constant, it is an interesting dynamic to think about. As both words, change and constant, seems to be completely opposite of each other. Change is referred to as dynamic and ever evolving, and constant means steady and regular. This phrase "change is the only constant" is used over and over in the business world of terminologies. Simply put, it means that the only thing constant in the world of business is change. It also means that as a business person you need to be willing and able to change your business paradigm and dynamics with the movement of the market. Another meaning pertains to your ability as a business person to let go of the past, its failures, successes, truths, prejudices, friends and enemies and not let your past interfere and dictate the future of your business and its viability in the marketplace. Being willing to change from a personal perspective and a business perspective, allows you as a business person to embrace the business world with open arms and being ready, willing and able to conquer the world.

SAY TO YOURSELF: I AM WILLING TO CHANGE AND MOVE FORWARD.

RULE # 88

I Am The Breadwinner

Being the breadwinner of a family comes with tremendous responsibilities and burdens, the breadwinner is the sole provider of their family, themselves and their dependents. Each member in a family is reliant on the breadwinner to provide for their survival and mere existence. Migrate that concept of a home breadwinner to a breadwinner of a business. As a breadwinner of a business, you are the only person responsible for the business existence and survival. You are solely responsible for the business failure or success. A breadwinner business person works diligently for the business, sacrificing personal enjoyment and pleasures, in exchange for fame and fortune, business growth and success. As a breadwinner, you have to be able to survive against all odds, swim in the turbulent business waters, seal deals with sharks, and constantly provide for your business and its growth.

SAY TO YOURSELF: I AM THE BREADWINNER OF MY BUSINESS AND MY BUSINESS IS MY RESPONSIBILITY.

RULE # 89

Being Ready

In the world of business, and everyday business transactions, like minded business persons are always ready, available, accessible and present. Being ready and present is part of the package of being a business person. Readiness is often referred to as making decisions on the spur of the moment, being able to attend business meetings without notice, being able to signs deals without forethought, and being able to stand firm and make a concerted business choice. Even though business persons are always ready and present, don't be fooled, they are not making erratic business decisions, these decisions are well thought of, calculated and strategic in nature. When the opportunities arise, business persons are ready and present. As a business person, you need to be ready and present, you need to condition your mind to be constantly in the present, always strategizing and being one step ahead of your business thoughts.

SAY TO YOURSELF: I AM ALWAYS READY AND PRESENT TO MAKE BUSINESS DECISIONS ON THE SPUR OF THE MOMENT.

RULE # 90

Be Your Own Brand Ambassador

Brand! Brand! Brand! Every business professor, magnate and leader, teaches brand recognition, brand identity and brand loyalty. Most of these brand courses and brand sessions hardly ever focus on branding of "You". As a business person, running your own business, working night and day to make it successful, toiling long hours when the world is asleep, seldom do you realize that there is no one else who knows your business better than you. Your best brand is You! Repeated again, Your best brand is You! Only you can sell your business, only you know your business inside out, only you can wine and dine and talk about your business with passion and dedication. You are your business, your business is you, and you are your own brand ambassador. Go out there and sell your business as you are the best sales representative, and command respect, for when your business name is mentioned, the next words mentioned should be your name. You and your business name should be interchangeable and synonymous.

SAY TO YOURSELF: MY BEST BRAND IS ME!

RULE # 91

The Need

Every idea is conceived firstly as a thought. It's like a seed implanted in the thought processes that festers and grows, never dissipating. This seed soon grows beyond control, being physically actioned and put into effect. This whole process of seed creation, to germination, to growth is equated to having a need and having the need fulfilled. Most, if not all business ideas are born out of a need to be fulfilled. Great thinkers envision needs in society, and envision the creation of products and services to solve specific problems emerging out of need. As a business person you must realize that your business is fulfilling a need that exist. The sooner you realize you are fulfilling that need in the market, the faster you are able to conceptualize the service and product you must create to fill the gap in the marketplace.

SAY TO YOURSELF: MY BUSINESS WILL FULFILL ITS INTENDED NEED IN THE MARKET.

RULE # 92

I Am The Driver

Drive, explore, learn, and grow. As drivers of your own destiny, you are responsible for your successes and your own personal growth. You can set your limits as achievable targets or unreachable targets. Once targets are set, they then become realistic and achievable. As a driver of your own destiny you are now steering the bus in the right direction. You are steering your life and business in the path which you require it to take. As a business person, you grab the steering wheel and drive your business to success. The same manner you steer your life, you steer your business. You need to realize that there are no limits to your abilities, so to, there are no limits to the number of stops you make along the way to your successes. Drive, explore, learn, capitalize and grow your business.

SAY TO YOURSELF: I AM THE DRIVER, DRIVING THIS BUSINESS.

RULE # 93

System And Process Everything

Looking around at the world, you would realize that the world is driven by systems and processes. Just think about it, ever act, every task, every product or service comes from something. This something is made up of systems and processes. Every product or service has a beginning and an end, it also had a middle ground.

This beginning, end, and middle are all part of systems and processes. Systems and processes are sequential steps of completing a task. The steps are so sequenced that the outcome is obvious and expected. Deviation from the system and process will produce abnormal results and in most cases non-conforming products and services. As a business person, once you get into the habit and make it a ritual, of using a system and applying processes to every task you undertake, you are on your way to becoming a success, as you have defined a pathway and a process to ensure your outcome and end result is achievable. Focus on managing the processes efficiently and effectively to achieve the systems that you put in place. Realize the value in implementing systems and processes as this helps streamline your business and reduce waste and inefficiencies.

SAY TO YOURSELF: I SEE VALUE IN SYSTEMS AND PROCESSES.

RULE # 94

The Perfect Client

The fallacy in the idea of the perfect client, is that every speaker, coach and business advisor, advises you to go after the perfect client. However in the world of business there is nothing like the perfect client. Clients and customers are not perfect, rather they are far from being perfect. Going after the perfect client in the business world simply put, means strategizing your business mindset to believe there is a client out there, that you would like to have and be able to conduct business with. As a business person, you need to create this perfect client, a client that only you can imagine would be a perfect fit for your business, a perfect masterpiece of your business puzzle that would allow you to grow your business exponentially. Once that perfect client is created, you then need to proceed to go in search of that perfect client. Once you begin to search for that perfect client that you want to strategize and grow with, you would soon realize that non-value added clients and clients who are not worth your effort and time will soon fall by the wayside, as you have a goal and a purpose and is set on achieving your goal and purpose.

SAY TO YOURSELF: MY PERFECT CLIENT AWAITS MY INTRODUCTION.

RULE # 95

Customer's Pain

A successful business person is always taking the time to understand their customers. Businesses often spend thousands of dollars on customer insight programs, trying to understand their customers. The reason they try to understand their customers, is the reason they remain in business. Understanding the customers and their pain or need is the surest way of a guaranteed business existence. As a business owner, you need to understand your customer's pain, you need to understand the way they feel, and the solution they are seeking. Once you understand their pain and the solution sought, you are better able to obtain, hold and retain, and secure a greater customer base. The whys of a customer existence and the whys of a customer need for your service will better assist you in your quest to understanding your customer's pain.

SAY TO YOURSELF: I UNDERSTAND MY CUSTOMER'S PAIN, AND I WILL RESOLVE THEIR PAIN.

RULE # 96

Assess The Competition

Every business owner, CEO, general manager, managing director and person in authority always takes time to assess the competition. Some even go to the extreme where they spy on, stalk, copy and steal from the competition. The world of business is a cut-throat type of world, it's an "every man for himself" type of business world, where only the strong survive. The weak and frail businesses fall by the sideline and the strong continue to monopolize and dominate the market. As a business owner, you need to constantly and continuously assess your competition. You need to place yourself in favourable positions where you can understand and see what the competition is doing all the time. You also need to be one step ahead of the competition. Hire the best people to work for you, treat them well and they will be loyal to you and your business. Always conduct a SWOT analysis (strengths, weakness, opportunities, and threats) of your business, ensuring you are positioning yourself well in the market place against your competition. Assess your competition all the time, never forget to pay special attention to your competition, because you competition is not forgetting you.

SAY TO YOURSELF: I WILL ASSESS MY COMPETITION ALL THE TIME.

RULE # 97

Have A Plan

The vision, the mission, the vision board, the jotted notes, the to-do list, and electronic reminders are all methods and ways of reminding oneself of tasks which need to be completed on a local and large scale, broad thinking, visionary level. Whether it is done on a locale minute level or a visionary upscale broad level, a plan needs to be put in place, so that the task becomes identifiable and achievable. A plan is a very important tool used by the most successful business people. Business people plan constantly, using various tools and methodologies. Successful planning allows for targets to be achieved, and deliverables to be met. Without a plan, the business is merely existing and utilising a lot of damage control methodologies along its growth path. As a business person, you need to have a plan, a defined plan with set targets, so that you can continue to grow your business while you strike off targets as they are achieved.

SAY TO YOURSELF: I HAVE A PLAN, AND I WILL ACTION MY PLAN DAILY.

RULE # 98

Don't Give Up

Some days are very tough, and you wonder why you bother to put your time and effort into a business that is not growing leaps and bounds like you wanted it to. The first thing that you must realize is that every day will never be the same, and that every customer you talk to will always have a concern and an issue that requires your resolution. Customers also will, in most cases require a manager or owner to provide resolution to their concern rather than speaking with front end staff. Your job as a business owner is to problem solve and keep the peace, provide solutions to concerns raised, and keep the process moving. It can become daunting, overwhelming and frustrating however you need to push ahead, with eyes to the sky and head held high. Don't give up, and don't let tasks overwhelm you. Look at each task and break it down to minute details which can be resolved piece by piece.

SAY TO YOURSELF: I WILL NOT GIVE UP, TODAY, TOMORROW OR ANY OTHER DAY.

RULE # 99

Visualize Your Finish Line Daily

In the world of business, it seems like tasks and people are always bombarding and surrounding you. It seems like every item and every task is urgent in nature and requires your immediate attention. Most business persons have priority task and a method to their madness which works, because most, if not all business owners are successful and gain recognition of their success by their deliverables. Deliverables are sometimes defined as the tasks to be listed, but once achieved, it becomes the end of the road, the finish line. The road seems less bumpy once you begin to visualize the finish line. Most tasks and duties are heavy and daunting, once you begin to break it done, you can see the end results being achieved.

SAY TO YOURSELF: EVERYDAY I SEE MY FINISH LINE, I AM ONE STEP CLOSER TO REACHING IT.

RULE # 100

Your Social Responsibility

As a business person you should strive to have a socially conscious business while you seek to capitalize your niche market. Businesses gain in reputation by being socially conscious, having that social responsibility and social allegiance to a social organization. Not only is the alliance between your business and the social organization acceptable, but it also helps to make your business visible within the social organization community and in turn enhances your business credibility. Customers delight in purchasing products and services from socially conscious organizations, because innately they feel, if a business can assist the growth of the community by being socially diligent, then that business deserves my hard-earned money. Being socially conscious and responsible is good, it builds your reputation, increases your revenue, and allows you to create a social brand for yourself.

SAY TO YOURSELF: MY SOCIAL RESPONSIBILITY IS TO MY COMMUNITY.

RULE # 101

Dream, Never Stop Dreaming

Accomplishments, initially comes from having dreams. Great thinkers, scholars, philosophers, inventors and business magnates each had a dream. Each followed their dream, and was never afraid to DREAM BIG or to STOP DREAMING. A life without dreams is a useless life, it is a life lacking value and purpose. Both the rich and the poor have dreams, the rich has the resources to make the dreams a reality, and the poor has the determination to succeed against all odds, the poor has nothing to lose, except a thought which was a dream, which never got actioned. Business persons never stop dreaming, they are always dreaming of bigger and better things for their business. As a business person, you cannot afford to stop dreaming, you need to dream and accomplish your dreams. Never stop dreaming, never give up, and most importantly NEVER STOP DREAMING ABOUT YOUR BUSINESS.

SAY TO YOURSELF: I AM NOT AFRAID TO DREAM, AND I WILL NEVER STOP DREAMING.

****

THANK YOU FOR READING.

I HOPE YOU IMPLEMENT WHAT YOU HAVE READ TO MAKE YOUR BUSINESS A SUCCESS.

****

ABOUT THE AUTHOR

Cindy Bahadur-Ramkumar is the CEO and Founder of Management Systems & Solutions. She has built and taught businesses how to operate, sustain and grow exponentially on zero (0) credit, streamlined and consolidated businesses, coached business owners how to maximize efficiencies and reduce cost all while maintaining a PROFIT.

Cindy is well known for creating structure in chaotic business environments while implementing strategic process improvements. She imparts the know-how on how to aspire to have your time equal more profit (time = more profit) and how to achieve profitable status as a business owner. She coaches and shows business owners how to think with purpose and create a pathway to profit.

Cindy is a Linguist (speaks 5 languages), Management System Auditor, Management Consultant by profession. She is also an Author, Reporter, Writer, Facilitator, Lecturer, Business Coach and Business Mentor.

To enhance your business potential visit www.mssconsultants.com, and email cindy@mssconsultants.com

www.ingramcontent.com/pod-product-compliance
Lightning Source LLC
Chambersburg PA
CBHW071801200526
45167CB00017B/983